**W9-AXY-798**

WITHDRAWN

BIOGRAPHY FROM
ANCIENT CIVILIZATIONS
LEGENDS, FOLKLORE, AND STORIES OF ANCIENT WORLDS

The Life and Times of

ARCHIMEDES

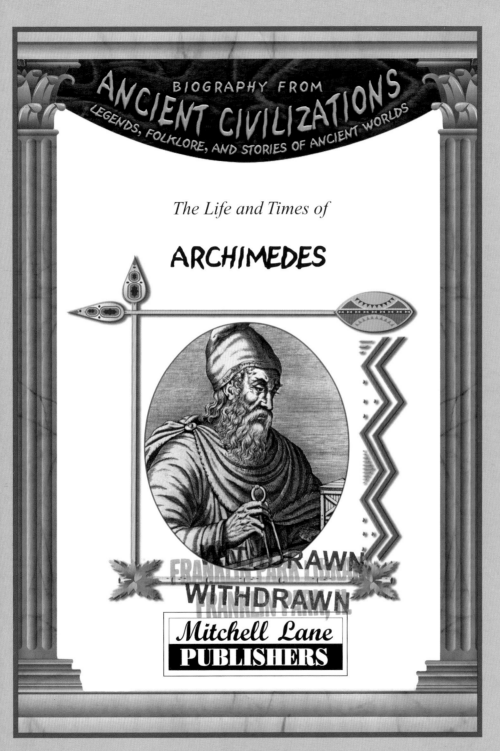

Mitchell Lane
PUBLISHERS

P.O. Box 196
Hockessin, Delaware 19707

BIOGRAPHY FROM
ANCIENT CIVILIZATIONS
LEGENDS, FOLKLORE, AND STORIES OF ANCIENT WORLDS

Titles
in the Series

The Life and Times of:

Alexander the Great
Archimedes
Aristotle
Augustus Caesar
Buddha
Catherine the Great
Charlemagne
Cicero
Cleopatra
Confucius
Constantine
Genghis Khan
Hammurabi

Herodotus
Hippocrates
Homer
Joan of Arc
Julius Caesar
King Arthur
Marco Polo
Moses
Nero
Pericles
Plato
Rameses the Great
Socrates

BIOGRAPHY FROM
ANCIENT CIVILIZATIONS
LEGENDS, FOLKLORE, AND STORIES OF ANCIENT WORLDS

The Life and Times of

ARCHIMEDES

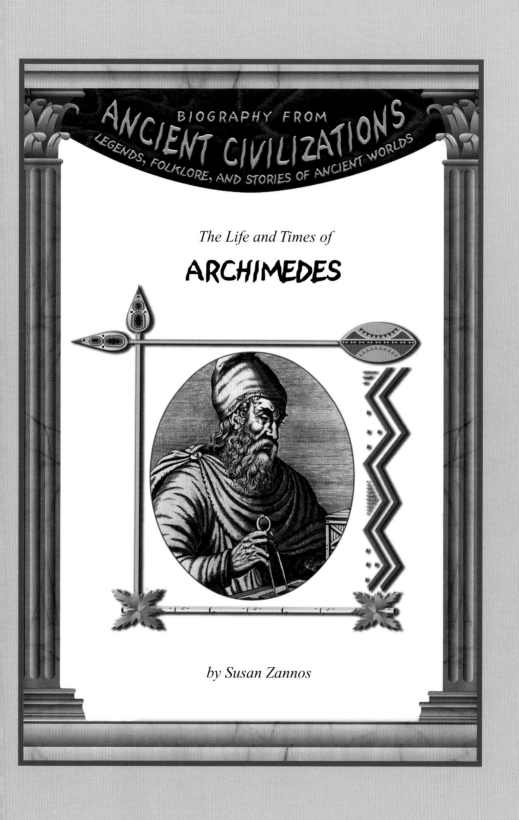

by Susan Zannos

Printing   3   4   5   6   7   8
Library of Congress Cataloging-in-Publication Data

Zannos, Susan.
   The life and times of Archimedes / Susan Zannos.
      p. cm. — (Biography from ancient civilizations)
   Includes bibliographical references and index.
   Contents: The golden wreath—How we know what we know—Alexandria—Syracuse—The siege.
   ISBN 1-58415-242-7 (lib. bdg.)
   1. Archimedes—Juvenile literature. 2. Scientists—Greece—Biography—Juvenile literature. [1. Archimedes. 2. Mathematicians. 3. Scientists. 4. Greece—Civilization—To 146 B.C.] I. Title. II. Series.
   Q143.A62Z36 2004
   509'.2—dc22
                                                                                2003024045
ISBN 13: 9781584-152422

ABOUT THE AUTHOR: Susan Zannos has been a lifelong educator, having taught at all levels, from preschool to college, in Mexico, Greece, Italy, Russia, and Lithuania, as well as in the United States. She has published a mystery *Trust the Liar* (Walker and Co.) and *Human Types: Essence and the Enneagram* (Samuel Weiser). Her book, *Human Types*, was recently translated into Russian, and in 2003 Susan was invited to tour Russia and lecture about her book. Another book she wrote for young adults, *Careers in Education* (Mitchell Lane) was selected for the New York Public Library's "Books for the Teen Age 2003 List." She has written many books for children, including *Chester Carlson and the Development of Xerography* and *The Life and Times of Ludwig van Beethoven* (Mitchell Lane). When not traveling, Susan lives in the Sierra Foothills of Northern California.

PHOTO CREDITS: Cover, pp. 1, 3, 6, 18, 28, 36, 40—Chris Rorres/Drexel University; pp. 9, 15—Corbis, p. 24—Getty Images; p. 34—Photo Researchers

PUBLISHER'S NOTE: This story is based on the author's extensive research, which she believes to be accurate. Documentation of such research is contained on page 47.

The internet sites referenced herein were active as of the publication date. Due to the fleeting nature of some web sites, we cannot guarantee they will all be active when you are reading this book.   PPH2,4

BIOGRAPHY FROM
ANCIENT CIVILIZATIONS
LEGENDS, FOLKLORE, AND STORIES OF ANCIENT WORLDS

The Life and Times of

ARCHIMEDES

            *For Your Information

Archimedes of Syracuse was one of the most famous mathematicians of the ancient world. He would concentrate so completely on thinking about mathematical problems that he would forget to eat and sleep. Although he preferred mathematical theory rather than practical applications, he created many useful inventions for King Hiero II of Syracuse.

CHAPTER
ONE

THE GOLDEN WREATH

Once upon a time in a beautiful island kingdom, a wealthy ruler wanted to make a special sacrifice to thank the gods for his good fortune. The king decided to have his royal goldsmith create a golden wreath as an offering to the gods. The king gave a bar of gold to the goldsmith. A month later this craftsman presented the king with a magnificent golden wreath made of golden leaves hammered fine and twined with golden ribbons. The wreath seemed light and lacey, a beautiful creation.

But wait a minute, thought the king. Maybe the wreath was too light. What if the goldsmith hadn't used all the gold? What if the man was dishonest and had taken some of the gold and replaced it with a less valuable metal like silver? The king was suspicious. He was afraid to make his offering to the gods—if it were not pure gold, the gods would know the difference. The king weighed the wreath. It weighed the same as the bar of gold had weighed. But the goldsmith might have added enough silver to make it weigh the same.

The king had a relative who was a mathematician and inventor. He sent for this man. "Archimedes," he said to his relative, "I have a problem that I need you to solve for me." King Hiero II told Archimedes that he suspected the goldsmith had cheated him. "How can I be sure that the wreath is pure gold?" he asked.

"That's simple," said Archimedes, "just melt it down. If the gold is of the same volume as the gold bar, then it is pure gold. If it is larger, then that means silver has been added."

"Oh no!" The king was horrified. He could not bear to have the beautiful wreath destroyed. "You will have to find a solution that does not harm the wreath."

"Well, I'll think about it," said Archimedes.[1]

He did think about it. First he tried to think of a way to measure all the shapes in the wreath, but he couldn't. The design was far too complicated. The leaves and ribbons were too thin and cleverly designed to be measured accurately. Archimedes thought and thought. He thought about the problem for a week. As was usual when he was concentrating on a difficult problem, he forgot to eat regularly. He forgot to sleep until he was so tired he fell asleep wherever he was sitting. He forgot to take a bath.

After a week was up, Hiero sent his servants to find Archimedes and bring him to the palace. The king's men found the mathematician under a shade tree near the city gates, drawing numbers and symbols in the dust with a stick. They brought him to the king.

"Have you figured out how to tell if the wreath is pure gold?" the king asked.

A well-known story about Archimedes claims that while he was in a public bath he noticed that when he got into the tub, water ran over the edge. From this he figured out how to tell the volume of a golden wreath by measuring how much water it displaced.

Archimedes shook his head. "Not yet," he said, "but I'm working on it."

"Phew!" said the king. "Archimedes, you smell bad! Really bad." He turned to the servants (who were standing a distance away because Archimedes did smell really bad). "Take him to the public baths and see to it that he gets clean."

The servants escorted Archimedes to the public baths. They filled a large tub with warm water clear up to the rim. They helped Archimedes take his clothes off and get into the tub. When Archimedes stepped into the tub, the water began spilling over the edge. He watched it drip onto the stone floor. He sat down in the tub. More water spilled over the edge. He watched it. He sank farther down, until only his eyes and the top of his head were out of the water, and watched still more water splash onto the floor.

"Eureka!" Archimedes shouted. (*Eureka* means "I have found it" in ancient Greek.) "Eureka!"[2] He ran out of the bath-house and down the street toward the palace. He was so excited he had forgotten to put his clothes on. He was stark naked.

What Archimedes had realized in the bath was that an object placed in water would displace an amount of water exactly equal to the size of the object. He explained this to the king (after he had put some clothes on) and asked for a large bowl filled with water to the brim. He set this bowl into a still larger bowl. Then he placed the golden wreath into the bowl of water. He very carefully measured the water that spilled out. Then he refilled the bowl and placed a bar of gold into it that was exactly the same size as the one given to the goldsmith. Again they measured the water that spilled out.

What did they find? They found that the wreath had displaced more water than the gold bar did. Therefore they knew that the size of the wreath was greater than the size of the gold bar. This meant that the goldsmith had taken some of the gold and then added silver until the weight of the wreath was the same as the weight of the original gold bar. Because silver weighs less than gold, the volume of the wreath was larger than the volume of the gold bar. Therefore it displaced more water.

The news of Archimedes' brilliant solution spread rapidly through the city. In fact, it spread so fast that it reached the sly goldsmith before the king's soldiers did. Since he had been clever enough to steal the gold (and he had been doing this sort of thing for quite a while without getting caught), he was certainly clever enough to get out of town fast, which he did.

Gold

Humans have valued the precious yellow metal, gold, for thousands and thousands of years. Archaeologists know that pharaohs in ancient Egypt used gold around 3000 B.C. Some experts claim that the first recorded discovery of gold was from 6000 B.C. in Mesopotamia. We do know that gold was first used as money in the Kingdom of Lydia (in what is now western Turkey) in 700 B.C.

In the ancient world gold was fashioned into brilliant wreaths, crowns, and ceremonial objects, in addition to ornaments and jewelry. During the medieval period, gleaming gold was used in religious icons, in mosaics on the walls and ceilings of churches, and in illustrated manuscripts. Of course it was displayed by powerful kings and princes. And in modern times, gold is still the material from which the finest jewelry is created.

The characteristics of gold make it easy to work with. Goldsmiths can press one ounce of gold into a thin sheet only five millionths of an inch thick to cover an area of 100 square feet. These thin sheets, called gold leaf, are used to cover objects of wood or plaster in a process called gilding. Gilded objects have the same luster and shine as objects of pure gold. One ounce of gold can be pulled into a wire 50 miles long, or used to cover a thin copper wire 1,000 miles long. Using gold to cover other metals with a very thin layer is called plating. It makes the other metals gleam like gold.

Gold is one of the heaviest metals, with a specific gravity of 19.3. This means that it weighs 19.3 times as much as an equal volume of water. One cubic foot of gold weighs more than half a ton. Throughout history there have never been any large robberies of gold bars (called gold bullion), probably because the robbers couldn't figure out how to carry it.

Another reason that gold is so valuable is that it is very scarce. The world's total supply of gold during all of recorded history to the present is only about 132,000 tons (120,000 metric tons). And it increases by only about 2,000 tons a year from gold mine production (remember that one cubic foot weighs more than half a ton). This means that all the gold in the world would fit into a cube 60 feet by 60 feet by 60 feet. It would be worth about one and a half trillion dollars.

In both his mathematical theories and his practical inventions, Archimedes made close observations and accurate measurements. Here he is shown measuring the city walls as he creates the defensive weapons that King Hiero requested. Although they were not used during the peaceful Hiero's reign, after the king's death Archimedes' weapons were used to defend Syracuse against Roman attack during the Punic Wars.

CHAPTER
TWO

HOW WE KNOW
WHAT WE KNOW

Is the story in the first chapter true? Well, that depends on what you mean by "true." Could it have happened? Yes. Is there any evidence that it happened? Yes. Did it happen just the way it was told? Probably not.

Archimedes lived over two thousand years ago. He was born in about 287 B.C. in the Greek city of Syracuse on the island of Sicily. He lived in Syracuse most of his life. He wrote many books about mathematics and astronomy, some of which still survive.

But he did not write about his own life.

Ancient sources say a writer named Heracleides, a friend of Archimedes, wrote a biography of him. If so, it has been lost. Perhaps some of the other writers who wrote about Archimedes used Heracleides' biography as a reference. Perhaps not. It isn't easy to be sure that books written two thousand years ago presented facts accurately. For one thing, writers then didn't have the same attitudes about facts.

Today, writers are careful to explain where they find their facts. If they get information from another writer, they tell who that other writer was. If they get information from interviews or from newspapers, they say so. Ancient writers felt free to borrow anything they wanted to from other people without saying where the material originated. As a result, we have no way of telling where the facts, the ideas, the stories about Archimedes came from. Some stories, such as the story about how Archimedes figured out if the wreath was solid gold, were told dozens of times and many different ways.

Vitruvius, a Roman architect who lived at the time of Emperor Augustus, told the story the first time that we know about. This was at the beginning of the Christian era. It was 200 years after Archimedes died. We could compare this story with stories we have about George Washington. About the same amount of time has passed between when George Washington lived and now as between when Archimedes lived and when Vitruvius wrote about him. Did George Washington cut down his father's cherry tree with his little hatchet? That story has been told dozens of times, too.

Even though we are much, much closer in time to George Washington than we are to Archimedes, we don't know whether the cherry-tree story is factual. Is there a sense in which it could be true without being completely factual? Many scholars think so. The point of the story about George Washington is that he was very honest. There is a lot of evidence that we are sure about that shows he was an honest man. So there is a sense in which the story is true even if it never happened.

The same kind of truth is found in the stories about Archimedes, both the ones that are fairly certain to be factual and

No one knows whether the famous story about George Washington chopping down a cherry tree is factual or not. In this painting it looks like he got caught before he had made much progress. Maybe he had already chopped down the cherry tree and was starting on another tree.

the ones that may not be. The stories show that he was one of the most brilliant mathematicians and one of the cleverest inventors who ever lived. There can be no doubt that this is true.

Of the ancient writers whose stories about Archimedes we have today, none actually lived at the same time as Archimedes. The closest was Polybius, a Greek who was born about 12 years after Archimedes died. Next came Cicero, a Roman who was born 100 years later. (Cicero went to Syracuse and found Archimedes' grave and cleaned it up.)[1] Next came Livy, a Roman born in 59 B.C.; and finally Plutarch, a Greek born around A.D. 45. After that the writers who wrote about Archimedes lived several hundred years later and used ancient writers for their sources.

Sometimes the sources they used have been lost, and sometimes they were written by the people just mentioned.

We don't know much about Archimedes' life when he was a boy, but we do know quite a bit about the world in which he lived. Syracuse, Archimedes' home, was one of the largest and most prosperous of the Greek cities. The city-states on the Greek mainland used to send out colonists as a kind of business venture. Wealthy citizens would finance the trip for adventurers who wanted to make their fortune. When these brave men were successful in establishing a colony, they would richly repay in trade and commerce the citizens who had sent them out.

In 734 B.C. the city of Corinth established such a colony on the southeast tip of the island of Sicily. The site had a natural harbor, fresh water, and was easy to defend. These advantages soon made the colony, Syracuse, one of the main ports of the western Mediterranean Sea. By the time Archimedes was born in the third century B.C., Syracuse was one of the largest Greek cities.

One of the few details that Archimedes mentioned about himself was that his father was an astronomer named Phidias. In one of his most important works, *The Sandreckoner*, Archimedes mentions that his father calculated the ratios of the diameters of the sun and moon. Plutarch states that Archimedes' family was related to Hiero II, who became king of Syracuse in 270 B.C.[2] This seems likely because Archimedes seems to have had a very close relationship with Hiero. Many of his most famous inventions were created for the king.

The period of Greek history when Archimedes lived was called the Hellenistic Period. (*Hellenes* was what the Greeks called themselves.) Greek civilization had been spread through-out the Mediterranean region by the conquests of Alexander of Macedon, known as Alexander the Great (356-323 B.C.). The Greeks were adventurers in many different ways. Alexander and his armies captured all of the known world (and then, legend says, he wept because there were no more worlds to conquer). Aristotle, Alexander's teacher, adventured into the realms of science and philosophy. Wherever Alexander went with his armies, he sent back specimens of animals and plants for his teacher to study.

The Greeks were curious. They were the first real scientists, eager to learn everything they could about the world. Because they were intellectual adventurers, they had a very great respect for education. They learned all they could about what others knew before making their own observations and experiments.

Archimedes would have attended school like other Greek boys, when he was about eight years old. The schools were less organized and official than schools are now. A pedagogue, or teacher, would teach a group of boys in his home. Often the school would go to the countryside to observe the natural world. The students would also have sport competitions: footraces, wrestling, throwing the discus. The Greeks knew that physical education was as important as intellectual education. The boys would also learn music and literature, memorizing poetry to recite as they played the lyre.

Phidias must have taken his son with him to study the stars and moon at night. The night sky over the beaches of Syracuse would have been like black velvet sprinkled with billions of brilliant stars. There were no electric lights in the ancient cities

Many of Archimedes most famous inventions involved the use of levers. By understanding the physical laws that enabled small amounts of force to move great weights with levers, Archimedes was able to move a huge, fully loaded ship from dry land to the sea. He said, "Give me a place to stand on, and I will move the earth."

to dim the splendor of the night. How big was the universe? How far away were the stars? The boy must have had nearly as many questions as there were stars. He would spend his entire life trying to answer them.

Greek Astronomy

Modern science began with the Greeks. They were the first to base their theories on close and accurate observations of nature. Like other ancient people, they were fascinated with the night sky. But unlike other people, the Greeks began to try to understand logically what the universe was like.

Long before the beginning of the Christian era, a Greek, Pythagoras (c.580–c.500 B.C.), had figured out that the earth was a sphere. He observed that most of the stars seemed to circle around a fixed point in the sky. He also observed that this point, where the North Star is located, was higher in the sky when he traveled northward. From this, and from the fact that ships seemed to disappear gradually over the horizon, he reasoned that the earth must be round. (It would take nearly 2,000 years before the idea that the earth is round became generally accepted.)

Pythagoras

Other stars, and some of the brightest ones, did not rotate around the North Star. They behaved strangely. They moved in about the same path across the sky used by the sun and moon. The Greeks called them "wanderers," or in the Greek language, *planetes,* and of course they are what we now know as planets. The Greeks gave these wandering stars the names of their gods. The moon was also thought to be a god. When, in the fifth century B.C., Anaxagoras claimed that the moon was similar to the earth, had hills and valleys, and shone with reflected light, he was sentenced to death for impiety. (Later his sentence was changed to exile.)

In the fourth century B.C. Heracleides observed the motions of the planets Mercury and Venus and suggested that they revolved around the sun—and that the earth did too. Not for more than two thousand years was this suggestion made again. Other attempts to explain the movements of the planets were more widely accepted. Aristotle (384–322 B.C.) stated that all the stars moved on crystal spheres with the sun at the center. He needed 55 different crystal spheres to describe all the complicated movements of stars and planets that he observed.

Aristarchus of Samos worked in Alexandria and was Archimedes' teacher. Much of his work was lost when the great library at Alexandria burned. What survived was his work measuring the sizes and distances of the sun and moon. Careful and precise measurements and mathematics, like those that Aristarchus used to develop his theories, became the foundation of the modern science of astronomy.

The lighthouse on the island of Pharos was one of the Seven Wonders of the Ancient World. For centuries it was the tallest structure in the world. Its gigantic mirror reflected the sun by day and fire by night. The light could be seen for more than 35 miles as it guided ships safely to the harbor of Alexandria.

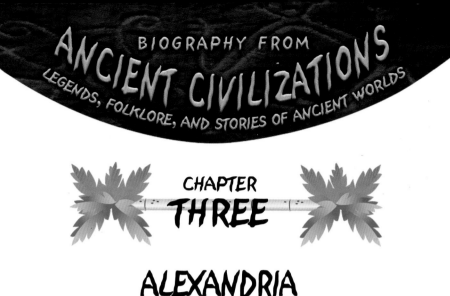
CHAPTER
THREE

ALEXANDRIA

Phidias must have been aware that his son Archimedes had a remarkable mind. The boy liked nothing better than to sit for hours trying to solve the mathematical problems his father gave him. And more often than not, he was successful. Phidias was determined that his son should have the best education possible. In the Hellenistic world, that meant going to Alexandria.

When Archimedes was a young man, King Hiero received the message from Ptolemy in Alexandria that the greatest scholars from all over the Greek world were welcome in Alexandria. Hiero spoke with Archimedes and offered his assistance. He was a wise king, and realized that an investment in genius would make a profitable return.

Alexander the Great had founded Alexandria in 332 B.C., after his conquest of Egypt. Located west of the Nile delta, it faced Greece across the Mediterranean. After Alexander's death, his general Ptolemy became ruler in Alexandria and made the city the intellectual and cultural capital of the Greek world. It became the largest metropolis. Ships came from all over the

Mediterranean Sea, guided safely to harbor by the Lighthouse of Pharos. This lighthouse was one of the Seven Wonders of the Ancient World. It was the world's tallest building and had a huge reflecting mirror that made its light visible for 35 miles.

Archimedes would have arrived in Alexandria by ship from Syracuse. He would have marveled at the lighthouse. Most certainly he would have climbed the tower to examine the amazing mirror that so intensified the sun's rays during the day and the light of a fire at night. Years later he would have a purpose for the knowledge he gained at the lighthouse.

What a time it was to be in Alexandria! It was the golden age of intellectual achievement. The best minds of the world were gathered there. Usually great discoveries are not made by isolated geniuses laboring alone. They are made by people working together, sometimes cooperating, sometimes competing. Great achievements occur when creative minds strike sparks from each other. The museum in Alexandria attracted the best and brightest in Greece. It was modeled on Plato's Academy and Aristotle's Lyceum, both from the fourth century B.C. in Athens. Alexandria was the main center of trade, as Athens had been previously.

Archimedes already had the reputation in his native Syracuse of being a bit strange. His habit of intense concentration when he was working on a mathematical problem caused some people to wonder if he was quite normal. In Syracuse he had been the ugly duckling. In Alexandria he found the other swans.

The mathematicians who gathered in the museum to study during the third century B.C. were the finest scientific minds of Greece. They studied the work of Euclid, who had lived in Alexandria before them. Euclid's great work on geometry, *The*

Elements, was known by all of them, and formed the foundation upon which their theories were built.

To many of us today, the names of those who made their remarkable discoveries in Alexandria at that time are dusty foot-notes in history books. But to themselves, it was the time of their lives. They had the friendship of others like themselves who were excited by science, who lived and breathed mathematical theories and observations about the heavens. It was work and study and argument and competition.

Archimedes met Conon of Samos in Alexandria, a young astronomer and mathematician who would become his lifelong friend. And Eratosthenes of Cyrene (which is now in Libya) was there, young and eager, teased by the others with the nickname Beta. They called him Beta, the second letter of the Greek alphabet, because they said that although he was good at many different things, he always came in second.

Archimedes knew, and learned from, the older astronomer and mathematician Aristarchus of Samos. We know from Archimedes' own account in *The Sandreckoner* that Aristarchus presented the theory that the sun, not the earth, was the center of the universe and that the earth and other planets revolved around the sun.

Conon, whose works have been lost, is sometimes credited with inventing the device called Archimedes' screw. His work on the curves in spirals seems closely related to this practical invention. Maybe he and Archimedes worked on it together. Maybe it happened when they were outside of Alexandria, walking and observing, talking and laughing, and proposing problems for each other to solve.

One of Archimedes' most famous inventions is the Archimedes screw, a device for raising water. (The invention is sometimes credited to Conon.) Since its invention around 250 B.C., it has been used until the present day. It was used in Egypt to irrigate fields, in Spain to empty the water from mines, and on board ships to bail out water. Today you can order one on the Internet.

As they walked near the river, they may have seen poor farmers carrying heavy buckets of water up the bank to irrigate their fields. All day long whole families worked together hauling the water for their crops, sweating under the hot Egyptian sun. "I'm glad I'm an astronomer and not a farmer," said Conon. "I'd hate to have to work that hard."[1]

"Nobody should work that hard," Archimedes agreed. "There has to be an easier way. Let's think about it. How could you get water to go from a lower level to a higher one without carrying it?" They found some sticks and began drawing diagrams in the soft mud. They thought of a waterwheel that would lift buckets of water with a continuous motion, but realized it would be too heavy to move from one field to another.

"The idea is less work," Conon said, "not more. I think it would have to be a pipe of some kind. Something inside a pipe that would draw the water up. What would do that?" They were

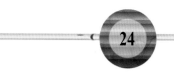

still bent over their mud blackboard with their sticks when the sun went down and they could no longer see the lines and figures they were drawing. It was a long walk back to Alexandria and the museum in the dark. When they arrived, they lit candles and continued their discussion far into the night.

The device known as Archimedes' screw—perhaps invented by one of them, perhaps the other, perhaps the two together—is still used in some parts of the world to irrigate fields. It consists of a spiral, like the threads on a screw, fitted inside a long cylinder. One end of the cylinder is put into the water. The spiral is turned with a crank, drawing the water up through the cylinder so that it spills out at the top. This invention had many other uses, such as clearing water from mines. The Romans used it in their Spanish mines (leading scholars to wonder whether Archimedes had ever visited Spain). And it was used to bail the water from ships caught in storms.

Maybe, while we're imagining scenes from Alexandria, the eager young Beta, Eratosthenes, proudly brought his results to Archimedes (who was nicknamed Alpha, number one) when he figured out the circumference of the earth:

"I know how big the earth is," he said.
"Hmmmm?" Archimedes mumbled, not looking up from the circles and angles he was drawing on a wax tablet.
"I know how big the earth is."
"That's good, Beta," Archimedes said, still not looking up. "How big is it?"
"The circumference of the earth is 25,750 miles."
"That seems bigger than I would have thought." Archimedes was looking at his young friend with interest now. "And how did you find this out?"

Eratosthenes told him how he had read in one of the library scrolls that there was a deep well in Syene (which is now Aswan). On the first day of summer, at exactly noon when the sun was directly overhead, its light shone all the way down into the well and reflected from the water. "So," he explained, " I put a long pole in the ground here at Alexandria, and I measured the shadow at exactly noon." He was then able to calculate the angle at the earth's center between Syene and Alexandria. He knew that this angle was about 1/50 of a circle. And he knew that the distance between Syene and Alexandria was about 515 miles. When he multiplied that distance times 50, the result had to be the circumference of the earth.

"You're sure you measured the angle of the shadow exactly?"

"I'm sure."

Archimedes shook his head in amazement. "That is an elegant piece of reasoning, Eratosthenes. I'll never call you Beta again!"

Eratosthenes' measurement was within 1 percent of being correct. He reasoned that it would be possible to reach India by sailing west from Spain. Not for another 1700 years would anyone test this idea—and Columbus might not have tried it if he had had Erastosthenes' figures on the circumference of the earth. Columbus thought the world was smaller than that.

For Archimedes, the golden days in Alexandria came to an end. It was time for him to return to Syracuse. He had been receiving polite enquiries from King Hiero. "Don't worry," he told his friends. "I'll write. I'll send you problems and proofs." It is because of these friendships, particularly his close friendship with Conon, that we have so many of Archimedes' theories and methods to study today. They were preserved because he sent them in letters to Alexandria throughout the rest of his life.

The Library at Alexandria

When Alexander the Great died, Ptolemy became ruler in Egypt. Ptolemy, and his son and grandson, made Alexandria the intellectual and cultural capital of the Greek world. They had the aim to collect all the books in the world in the library of Alexandria.

When the books were written in other languages, scholars translated them into Greek. Seventy-two rabbis, all Jewish scholars, were brought to Alexandria by Ptolemy I to translate the Old Testament from Hebrew into Greek.

Ptolemy III sent letters to kings all over the world asking to borrow their books. When Athens, for example, sent the texts of her great tragic poets Aeschylus and Sophocles, Ptolemy had them copied. He then kept the originals and sent the copies back to Athens. All the ships that stopped at Alexandria were searched for books. These books received the same treatment. While these methods came close to being robbery, they resulted in a magnificent library with hundreds of thousands of books.

Scholars came to Alexandria to work on translations and to organize the special collections devoted to mathematics, science, literature, astronomy, medicine, and other divisions of knowledge. A museum was built near the library. It housed the scholars who came to study and work at the library. There was an observatory on the second level, and classrooms all around it. Located near the royal palace grounds, it was surrounded by gardens and a zoo with animals from all over the known world.

The actual shelves consisted of pigeonholes for the scrolls. The most important scrolls were wrapped in linen or leather jackets to protect them. The first of the librarians was Demetrius of Athens, who had been a student of Aristotle. At that time most libraries were simply the collections of manuscripts owned by private persons. Ptolemy I gave Demetrius the job of contacting the people known to possess such collections and convince them to let him have their books copied.

The next librarian was Callimachus of Cyrene, who created a subject catalog of 120,000 of the library's collection using Aristotle's divisions of knowledge. Not everything was cataloged. Next came Eratosthenes, mathematician and friend of Archimedes, who compiled what he called a scheme of the bookshelves. Our libraries today, with their computerized catalogs and shelves organized by call letters on the spines of books, had their beginnings over two thousand years ago in Alexandria.

Unfortunately, at least part of the library burned when Roman general Julius Caesar conquered the city in 48 B.C. Within a few hundred years, the entire library was gone.

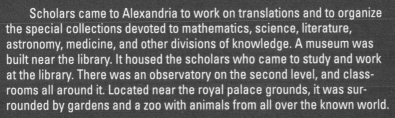

After the Romans had captured Syracuse, the conquering general, Marcellus, sent soldiers to bring Archimedes to him, ordering them not to harm the old mathematician. Marcellus had great respect for Archimedes, even though the weapons he had invented prevented Rome from an easy victory. The soldiers found Archimedes so deeply in thought that he did not hear them coming.

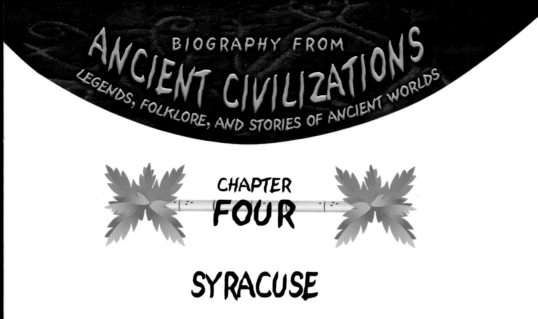
CHAPTER

FOUR

SYRACUSE

Back in Syracuse, Archimedes settled into the activities that would occupy him for the rest of his life. On the one hand he had requests and commissions from King Hiero. On the other hand he had his own interests, which were concerned with mathematical theories. The king did not at all understand what Archimedes was doing with the diagrams and numbers that he was constantly drawing. He wanted to see practical results. Fortunately, Archimedes and the king were good friends. They liked each other even if they didn't always understand each other.

What Archimedes liked best was mathematical theory, not practical inventions. He would become so fascinated with problems of geometry that he'd forget everything else. Plutarch described the situation:

> Oftimes Archimedes' servants got him against his will to the baths, to wash and anoint him, and yet being there, he would ever be drawing out of the geometrical figures, even in the very embers of the chimney. And while they were anointing of him with oils and sweet savours, with

his fingers he drew lines upon his naked body, so far was he taken from himself, and brought into ecstasy or trance, with the delight he had in the study of geometry.[1]

Once Archimedes had solved a problem, he would send it to Conon and his other friends in Alexandria so that they could work on it and solve it, too. They could give the theorems to their students. Sometimes Archimedes would wait quite a while before sending the solution, or proof, of the problem to Alexandria. Some of the younger mathematicians there weren't entirely honest. They would claim that they had discovered the theorems themselves.

In the preface to one of his works, *On Spirals*, Archimedes tells how he tricked those who tried to steal his work. He had included two false theorems in his previous letter, "so that those who claim to discover everything, but produce no proofs of the same, may be confuted as having pretended to discover the impossible."[2]

Many of Archimedes' works have been lost. But the ones that we have show that he was one of the greatest mathematicians of all time. It is very difficult for mathematical scholars to read the works of Archimedes, and impossible for the rest of us. This is because he didn't have the numerals that we have to represent numbers. He had to use the letters of the Greek alphabet, and other symbols. To understand his work you have to be not only a very good mathematician yourself, but also able to read Greek in the form used over two thousand years ago, and you have to know how the Greek letters were used to represent numbers. And then you have to be able to do the math!

One of his works, *The Sandreckoner*, is quite astonishing. In it, Archimedes calculates the number of grains of sand that it would take to completely fill up the universe. No wonder King Hiero kept asking him to be practical! Maybe it was to keep Hiero happy that Archimedes dedicated *The Sandreckoner* to Hiero's son Gelo. In this work, Archimedes first explains the size of the grains of sand—a lot less than the size of a poppy seed. So he was imagining very, very small grains. Why? Because he wasn't really interested either in sand or in the size of the universe. What he was doing was explaining how to solve the problem of writing very large numbers.

The Greeks had only letters and words to use as symbols for numbers. They had no concept of zero. This made it impossible to work with very large numbers until Archimedes worked out his ideas in *The Sandreckoner*. This book is interesting for other reasons as well. One is that it gives the theory of Aristarchus that the sun, not the earth, is the center of the solar system. Curiously enough, Archimedes didn't take this idea seriously. He only used it to show that even if the universe were many times larger than people thought, he could still calculate a number for the grains of sand it would take to fill it up.

Of his other works, such as *On Plane Equilibrium, On Spirals,* and *On Floating Bodies,* the one of which Archimedes was proudest was *On the Sphere and Cylinder.* In it he shows that the volume of a sphere is two-thirds the volume of the cylinder that contains it. He shows that the surface of the sphere is two-thirds the surface of the cylinder, including its bases. He was so pleased with this work that he said he wanted the figure of a sphere within a cylinder placed on his gravestone.

Meanwhile, his friend King Hiero just shook his head when Archimedes told him about spheres and cylinders, spirals and parabolas, and the number of grains of sand that would fill up the universe. "What good is that?" Hiero would ask. "I need practical results. I need machines that can get some work done. I need things that will impress people."

So Archimedes made the king wonderful things. And the things he made certainly impressed people. The machines Archimedes made caused his fame to spread all over the Greek and Roman world.

Archimedes made a planetarium that showed the movements of the sun and moon and all the planets. Each of the heavenly bodies revolved in its own orbit around the earth. The fixed stars, all of the constellations, were on the largest sphere of all. When he turned a small crank, the whole universe revolved in accurate motions. It was such a wonder that many ancient writers told about it. But Archimedes didn't write about it. He just wasn't interested in the practical applications of his theories.

Another time, Archimedes was explaining to the king about how levers could make work easier by lifting large weights with a small amount of effort. He said to the king, "Give me a place to stand on, and I will move the earth."[3]

The king decided to test Archimedes. Hiero loved big projects that would impress people. He had just had a huge ship built, the *Syracusia*. It weighed 4,200 tons. It was filled with every luxurious item the king could think of. He intended it as a gift for King Ptolemy of Egypt. The huge ship with three tall masts, fully loaded, sat on the beach. All the king's slaves

working together could not move it. The king asked Archimedes to launch the ship.

There are many different accounts of exactly what machines Archimedes used—most writers seem to think he constructed a complicated series of pulleys (ropes passing over wheels) of different sizes. When he was finished, he gave the end of the rope to the king and told him to pull it. To everyone's astonishment, when the king gave a slight tug on the rope, the ship began to move as easily as if it were floating on water. It glided like magic down to the sea and into the water. King Hiero called out, "From this day forth, Archimedes is to be believed in everything he may say."[4]

Archimedes served the king in many other practical ways. There was of course the matter of the golden wreath and the dishonest goldsmith. Archimedes was so excited about that solution that he ran through the streets naked, shouting, "Eureka!" And he didn't stop with just figuring out that problem. He went on to study the weights of objects in water, and to compare those weights with the weights of objects in air. The result of this study was to arrive at what is called the specific gravity of different elements. This method has been used in the study of chemistry ever since.

King Hiero also asked Archimedes to make different kinds of weapons to defend the city. Hiero was a wise and good king to his people, not one who was always fighting wars. Archimedes didn't understand what the king wanted all the weapons for, but because he liked and respected the king, he made them anyway. As it turned out, Archimedes would be as famous for the weapons he designed as for any of his other marvelous inventions.

This 16th Century illustration represents two different types of arithmetic. The Greek mathematician Pythagoras who lived in the 6th Century B.C. is shown with an abacus, a device that is still used for calculating in many parts of the world today. On the other side of the picture, Boethius, a Roman philosopher, uses the Arabic numerals and symbols that we use to learn arithmetic in our schools.

Numerals

It was difficult to arrive at a system of symbols that would stand for numbers. It was easier to evolve symbols that stood for sounds. Letters for writing words developed a thousand years before our system of numerals appeared. In fact, in many parts of the world, letters were used for a long time as symbols for numbers.

The first method of writing down numbers was a tally system. One mark meant one cow—or whatever it was you were counting. Some tally systems were quite complicated, like the one in Babylonia that was based on units of 60. We still have the remnants of this system in the number of degrees in a circle, and in the way we tell time: 60 minutes to an hour, 60 seconds to a minute.

The ancient Hebrews used an alphabetic system. The first nine letters stood for one through nine, the second nine letters for 10 through 90, and the third nine letters for 100 through 900. This meant they needed 27 symbols, and the Hebrew alphabet only had 22 letters. They filled in the last five with special forms of letters that occurred only at the ends of words. Numbers were figured by adding the symbols together. If we did this with the English alphabet, we would write the number 444 as VMD. V stands for 400, M for 40, and D for 4. When you add together 400 + 40 + 4, you get 444.

The earliest system of numerals in Greek worked the way Roman numerals do. In Roman numerals, 1 = I, 5 = V, 10 = X, 50 = L, 100 = C, 500 = D, and 1000 = M. In this system it was possible to subtract one unit by placing it to the left of a larger unit. Therefore three is written III, but four is written IV (five minus one). Eighty is written LXXX (fifty plus three tens), but ninety is written XC (one hundred minus ten).

In Alexandria during the third and second centuries B.C., Greek mathematicians began using an alphabetic system of numerals similar to the Hebrew system. When the Greeks intended a letter to be used as a number, they placed a small line like an accent mark after it. The problem with all of these early systems was a big one: there was no symbol for zero. This meant that they had no way to write very large numbers, such as 1,000,000. This made it extremely difficult for their astronomers to figure out the huge distances between heavenly bodies.

Not until the concept of zero was borrowed from Arab mathematicians—who had in turn borrowed it from India—did Europeans have a system of numerals flexible enough to handle very large numbers.

According to legend, one of the wonderful weapons that Archimedes created for the defense of Syracuse was a huge mirror composed of hundreds of tiny mirrors. With this he was able to focus and concentrate the rays of the sun so intensely that the enemy ships would burst into flame. Perhaps he learned this technique from studying the mirror in the Lighthouse of Pharos.

BIOGRAPHY FROM ANCIENT CIVILIZATIONS

LEGENDS, FOLKLORE, AND STORIES OF ANCIENT WORLDS

CHAPTER FIVE

THE SIEGE

In the third century B.C., two great powers, Rome and Carthage, began fighting. Their conflicts were called the Punic Wars. Rome, the capital of Italy, was on the northern side of the Mediterranean Sea. Carthage was on the coast of Africa on the southern side of the Mediterranean Sea. Sicily, with the city of Syracuse, was right in the middle. Of course both Rome and Carthage wanted control of Syracuse.

While Hiero was king in Syracuse, he managed to stay out of the war. With clever diplomacy he first allied himself with Carthage and later signed a peace treaty with Rome. But when Hiero died in 215 B.C., things fell apart fast. Rome and Carthage were still at war. Hiero's son Gelo had died the previous year. Hiero's grandson, Hieronymos, became king when he was only 15 years old. The boy was not old enough to control the explosive situation. He and other members of Hiero's family were assassinated in 214 B.C. The men who took control in Syracuse were on the side of Carthage.

Rome sent one of their best soldiers, Marcellus, to capture Syracuse. Plutarch described Marcellus as being "by long experience, skilful in the art of war, of a strong body, valiant of hand, and by natural inclinations addicted to war."[1] Marcellus thought it would be easy to capture the city. He knew that Syracuse had been at peace for a long time. He thought that the citizens would not know how to defend their city. Marcellus sent forces commanded by another general to attack Syracuse on the landward side. He himself commanded 60 huge ships, called galleys, loaded with weapons. Marcellus thought that he could capture Syracuse in a week at most. He might have been right, except that he had forgotten about one old man.

According to Polybius, the Romans "failed to reckon with the talents of Archimedes or to foresee that in some cases the genius of one man is far more effective than superiority in numbers. This lesson they now learned by experience."[2]

Of the many accounts of the battle for Syracuse, and of the wonderful weapons devised by Archimedes, the one by Polybius (c.200–c.118 B.C.) is the oldest. Although he was not yet born when the siege took place, Polybius had the advantage of talking with eyewitness survivors from Syracuse. He also had access to the official Roman accounts.

The weapons that Archimedes had created for his friend King Hiero years before were ready and waiting. The people of Syracuse, made brave by the calm, clear explanations Archimedes gave them, followed his orders in operating the machines.

When Marcellus's ships approached Syracuse, some sources say Archimedes used a huge mirror constructed of hundreds of tiny mirrors. Perhaps it was similar to the great mirror in the lighthouse at Alexandria. The mirrors focused the rays of the sun on the wooden ships with such intensity that the ships burst into flame. Other ships came closer. Archimedes responded with catapults that hurled stones of enormous weight, crushing the ships that they hit. Still other ships came too close to the shore for the big stones to hit them. For these, long beams swung out, and grappling hooks were lowered on chains. The hooks grabbed onto the prows of the ships like big claws. The chains were drawn up, lifting the ships out of the water like toys. The sailors on the ships fell into the sea. Then the hooks let go. The ships crashed into the sea, capsizing and sinking.

Similar grappling hooks were used on the landward side. When Roman soldiers attempted to come near the wall of the city, hooks were lowered that picked them up, raised them into the air, and dropped them. Archimedes also made holes in the city walls so that men could stand behind them, protected, while they shot at the Romans with small catapults and bows and arrows. The Roman soldiers became so frightened by Archimedes' weapons that they would panic every time a stick or piece of rope appeared over the wall. They thought it was some new terrible device and ran away. Marcellus asked whether Archimedes "by the multitude of missiles that he hurls at us all at once outdoes the hundred-armed giants of mythology."[3]

Finally the Romans gave up their efforts to take Syracuse by force. Polybius wrote, "So long as he was present they did not dare even to attempt an attack by any method which made it possible for Archimedes to oppose them."[4] Marcellus decided that the Romans would blockade Syracuse and starve the people into surrendering. While waiting, Marcellus and his troops

The Roman soldiers sent by Marcellus ordered Archimedes to come with them to meet the general. Archimedes was so lost in concentration on a mathematical problem that he did not look up. He had been drawing diagrams in the sand and asked the soldiers not to disturb the figures he was creating. Enraged because he did not obey their orders, the soldiers stabbed Archimedes.

destroyed most of the other cities of Sicily that were on the side of Carthage.

Eventually the Romans noticed that one section of the wall around Syracuse was not carefully guarded. They managed to sneak into the city at night and sound trumpets so that the citizens thought the whole city had been taken. While panic seized the population, Roman soldiers poured in and took control. Marcellus felt pity for the beautiful city, but he could not keep the soldiers from looting and destroying Syracuse. He gave orders that no one was to harm Archimedes, but it did no good.

Archimedes was so intent on solving one of his mathematical problems that he did not even realize that the city had fallen. According to one account by Plutarch, a soldier came upon Archimedes and commanded him to come with him to Marcellus. The old mathematician told the soldier not to disturb the diagram he was drawing and to wait until he had finished his calculations. The soldier was enraged because the old man did not obey. He drew his sword and killed Archimedes.

Marcellus was very sad when he heard that his noble opponent had been killed. He saw to it that Archimedes received a proper burial. The gravestone that Archimedes had requested, a figure of a sphere enclosed in a cylinder, was placed on his grave. When Cicero went to Sicily over a century later, he searched for Archimedes' grave:

> [I] found it enclosed all around and covered with brambles and thickets; for I remembered certain doggerel lines inscribed, as I had heard, upon his tomb, which stated that a sphere along with a cylinder had been put on top of his grave. . . . I noticed a small column arising a little above the bushes, on which there was a figure of a sphere and a cylinder.[5]

Cicero had slaves clear the grave of weeds, clean it up, and take care of it.

The real memorial to Archimedes was not carved in stone. It was not even the many stories told about his marvelous inventions. It was his dedication to understanding the pure realm of theoretical mathematics, and the theorems he left for those mathematicians who would study them throughout the centuries.

FYI
For Your Info

The Punic Wars

By the third century B.C., Carthage controlled most of North Africa and southern Spain, and the islands of Sardinia and Corsica. The Carthaginians were very wealthy and powerful. Meanwhile, Rome's power increased until it reached the southern tip of Italy. In between the two great powers lay the island of Sicily. They both wanted it.

The First Punic War began in 264 and took place entirely in Sicily. Rome laid siege to cities controlled by Carthage in western Sicily. Carthage sent its navy to the aid of the cities, and the Romans destroyed the navy. For the first time in its history, Carthage no longer controlled the sea. After 23 years of conflict, Rome and Carthage signed a peace treaty in which Carthage gave up its claim to Sicily.

Three years later, in 238 B.C., the Romans seized the island of Corsica. Without their navy, the Carthaginians weren't prepared to do anything about it immediately. Instead, they sent their best generals to Spain to form colonies and an army. By 221 B.C., Hannibal assumed command in Spain. When one of the Spanish cities revolted and asked Rome for help, Hannibal destroyed the city. Rome demanded that Hannibal be removed from Spain. Carthage refused. The Second Punic War began in 218 B.C.

By this time Carthage had created a powerful empire in Spain, with a large army. The brilliant young Hannibal marched this army, complete with elephants, north from Spain. He then headed south, crossing the Alps into northern Italy, where he defeated the Roman armies. Within two months he had conquered northern Italy. Roman allies in the south of Italy joined Carthage. So did the island of Sicily. But Rome still controlled the sea and sent General Marcellus to capture Syracuse.

Rome finally got smart. Instead of confronting Hannibal in battle, they cut him off from his supplies by conquering Spain. Hannibal won every battle with the Romans, but he lost the war. The Romans crossed the Mediterranean from Spain to North Africa and reduced Carthage to a dependent state. The result of the Second Punic War was the complete domination of the known world by Rome.

The Third Punic War was not so much a war as a three-year massacre. The Roman Senate declared war in 149 B.C. Rome attacked Carthage and destroyed it, killing or selling into slavery all the inhabitants. The Romans destroyed the city and the harbor. They sowed the surrounding country with salt so that it would never again be inhabitable.

Surviving Works by Archimedes

Measurement of a Circle
On Conoids and Spheroids
On Floating Bodies
On Plane Equilibriums
On the Sphere and Cylinder
On Spirals
On the Method of Mechanical Problems
Quadrature of the Parabola
The Sandreckoner

Timeline in History

332 B.C.	Alexander the Great founds Alexandria in Egypt
323	Death of Alexander the Great; Ptolemy I rules in Alexandria
322	Death of Aristotle
300	Euclid writes *The Elements*
295	Ptolemy I begins collecting books for library at Alexandria
290	Construction of the Lighthouse of Alexandria begins
287	Birth of Archimedes in Syracuse; Ptolemy II becomes king of Alexandria
270	Hiero is declared king of Syracuse; Birth of Hiero's son Gelo
264	The First Punic War begins

Timeline in History

263 B.C.	Hiero signs peace treaty with Rome
246	Ptolemy III becomes king of Alexandria
245	Callimachus of Cyrene becomes librarian at Alexandria, creates a subject catalog
240	Gelo begins co-rule with Hiero in Syracuse
241	End of First Punic War
230	Birth of Hiero's grandson, Gelo's son, Hieronymos
235	Eratosthenes becomes librarian at Alexandria, calculates circumference of the earth
220	Death of Archimedes' friend Conon, astronomer and mathematician
218	Second Punic War begins; Hannibal crosses the Alps and invades Italy
216	Death of Gelo in Syracuse
215	Hiero dies and Hieronymos becomes king of Syracuse
214	Hieronymos and members of his family are assassinated
213	Marcellus attacks Syracuse but is defeated by Archimedes' weapons
212	Syracuse falls to Romans commanded by Marcellus; death of Archimedes
208	Marcellus killed by Hannibal's forces
201	End of Second Punic War
200	Birth of Polybius, Greek historian who wrote about Archimedes' inventions
183	Death of Hannibal, who commits suicide to avoid capture by Romans
180	Aristarchus, who stated that the earth revolved around the sun, becomes librarian at Alexandria
146	Carthage utterly destroyed by Rome

Chapter Notes

CHAPTER ONE   THE GOLDEN WREATH

1. E. J. Dijksterhuis, *Archimedes* (Princeton, N.J.: Princeton University Press, 1987), p. 19.

2. Ibid.

CHAPTER TWO   HOW WE KNOW WHAT WE KNOW

1. J. J. O'Connor and E. F. Robertson, *Archimedes of Syracuse* (University of St. Andrews, Scotland: http://www-groups.dcs.st-and.ac.uk/~history/Mathematicians/Archimedes.html, p. 6.

2. Plutarch, *The Lives of the Noble Grecians and Romans* (New York: Modern Library), p. 376.

CHAPTER THREE   ALEXANDRIA

1. Author's retelling of events and conversation that could have taken place based on her extensive research.

CHAPTER FOUR   SYRACUSE

1. Plutarch, *The Lives of the Noble Grecians and Romans* (New York: Modern Library), p. 378.

2. J. J. O'Connor and E. F. Robertson, *Archimedes of Syracuse* (University of St. Andrews, Scotland: http://www-groups.dcs.st-and.ac.uk/~history/Mathematicians/Archimedes.html, p. 1.

3. E. J. Dijksterhuis, *Archimedes* (Princeton, N.J.: Princeton University Press, 1987), p. 15.

4. Ibid.

CHAPTER FIVE   THE SIEGE

1. Plutarch, *The Lives of the Noble Grecians and Romans* (New York: Modern Library), p. 378.

2. Drexel University: Archimedes (http://www.mcs.drexel.edu/~crorres/Archimedes/contents.html), p. 1.

3. Plutarch, *The Lives of the Noble Grecians and Romans* (New York: Modern Library), p. 378.

4. Drexel University: Archimedes (http://www.mcs.drexel.edu/~crorres/Archimedes/contents.html), p. 3.

5. J. J. O'Connor and E. F. Robertson, *Archimedes of Syracuse* (University of St. Andrews, Scotland: http://www-groups.dcs.st-and.ac.uk/~history/Mathematicians/Archimedes.html, p. 6.

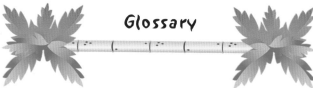

Glossary

anoint	(ah-NOYNT) to apply oil or ointment
assassinate	(ah-SASS-ah-nayt) to kill someone of political importance by violence
astronomy	(ah-STRAH-no-mee) the science of celestial bodies
blockade	(blah-KAYD) an attempt to starve an enemy to surrender by preventing supplies from entering the enemy's settlement
calculate	(KAL-kew-layt) to solve using mathematics
capsize	(KAP-size) to turn over in the water
catapult	(KAT-ah-puhlt) a machine for hurling giant stones
colony	(KAH-luh-nee) a place settled by people from another country
impiety	(im-PYE-eh-tee) lack of respect for the gods
looting	(LOO-ting) stealing things after winning a battle
metropolis	(meh-TRAH-po-lihs) a very large city, usually a capital city
numeral	(NEW-mur-uhl) a symbol standing for a number
observatory	(ub-ZER-vuh-tor-ee) a room or building for studying celestial bodies
papyrus	(pah-PYE-rus) paper made of a type of grass that grows along the Nile River of Africa
parchment	(PARCH-ment) paper made of goat or sheep skin
planetarium	(plan-uh-TARE-ee-um) a room in which a model of the solar system can be projected
siege	(SEEDJ) the attack of a city or country in a way that prevents supplies or reinforcements from entering
sphere	(SFEER) three-dimensional circular shape, such as a ball
spiral	(SPY-rul) a curved shape like a bedspring or a snail shell
symbol	(SIM-bul) a sign or object representing something
theorem	(THEER-um) a rule that can be logically proven
treaty	(TREE-tee) an agreement between countries

For Further Reading

For Young Adults

Gardner, Martin. *Archimedes: Mathematician and Inventor.* New York: The Macmillan Company, 1965.

Ipsen, D. C. *Archimedes: Greatest Scientist of the Ancient World.* Hillside, N.J.: Enslow Publishers, Inc., 1988.

Jonas, Arthur. *Archimedes and His Wonderful Discoveries.* Englewood Cliffs, N.J.: Prentice Hall, Inc., 1963.

Lafferty, Peter. *Archimedes.* New York: The Bookwright Press, 1991.

Lexau, Joan M. *Archimedes Takes a Bath.* New York: Thomas Y. Crowell Company, 1969.

On the Internet

Bede's Library: "The Mysterious Fate of the Great Library of Alexandria" http://www.bede.org.uk/library.htm

Drexel University: *Archimedes* http://www.mcs.drexel.edu/~crorres/Archimedes/contents.html

O'Connor, J. J., and E. F. Robertson. *Archimedes of Syracuse.* University of St. Andrews, Scotland: http://www-groups.dcs.st-and.ac.uk/~history/Mathematicians/Archimedes.html

Works Consulted

Dijksterhuis, E. J. *Archimedes.* Princeton, N.J.: Princeton University Press, 1987.

Perkins, David. *Archimedes' Bathtub: The Art and Logic of Breakthrough Thinking.* New York: W. W. Norton & Company, 2000.

Plutarch. *The Lives of the Noble Grecians and Romans.* New York: Modern Library, no copyright.

Index